FAMILY Life ISSUES

Growing as a
Christian
Mother

Written by Elaine Bickel

D1096716

CPH™
SAINT LOUIS

Edited by Rodney L. Rathmann

Editorial assistant: Phoebe W. Wellman

Write to Library for the Blind, 1333 S. Kirkwood Road, St. Louis, MO 63122-7295 to obtain *Growing as a Christian Mother* in braille or in large print for the visually impaired. Allow six months for processing.

Unless otherwise stated, the Scripture quotations in this publication are from THE HOLY BIBLE: NEW INTERNATIONAL VERSION®. Copyright © 1973, 1978, 1984 by International Bible Society. Used by permission of Zondervan Publishing House. All rights reserved.

The "NIV" and "New International Version" trademark are registered in the United States Patent and Trademark Office by International Bible Society. Use of either trademark requires the permission of International Bible Society.

Copyright © 1994 Concordia Publishing House
3558 South Jefferson Avenue, St. Louis, MO 63118-3968
Manufactured in the United States of America

1 2 3 4 5 6 7 8 9 10   03 02 01 00 99 98 97 96 95 94

Contents

Introduction

▲ How to Use This Course

This course has been especially prepared for use in small group settings. It may, however, also be used as a self-study or in a traditional Sunday morning Bible class.

▲ Planning for a Small Group Study

1. *Select a leader* for the course or a leader for the day. It will be the leader's responsibility to secure needed materials, to keep the discussion moving, and to help involve everyone.

2. *Emphasize sharing.* Your class will work best if the participants feel comfortable with one another and if all feel that their contributions to the class discussion are important and useful. Take the necessary time at the beginning of the course to get to know one another. You might share names, occupations, hobbies, etc. Share what you expect to gain from this course.

Invite participants to bring photos of their families to the first session to pass around as they introduce themselves and tell about the individual members of their families. Be open and accepting. Don't force anyone to speak. The course will be most helpful if participants willingly share deep feelings, problems, doubts, fears, and joys. That will require building an atmosphere of openness, trust, and caring among one another. Take time to build relationships among participants. That time will not be wasted.

3. Help participants apply the concepts included in each session. After each week's study, there is a list of suggested activities. An old Chinese proverb summarizes the "why?" of doing these activities during the week:

I hear and I forget;
    I see and I remember;
        I do and I understand.

The activity is to help participants do and thus understand. Encourage everyone to take time to do them.

4. Encourage participants to invite their friends—including their unchurched friends—to be a part of this study.

▲ As You Plan to Lead the Group

1. Read this guide in its entirety before you lead the first session.

2. Use the Leaders Notes found in the back of this guide.

3. Pray each day for those who join the group.

4. As you prepare for each session, study the Bible texts thoroughly. Work through the exercises for yourself. Depend on the Holy Spirit. Expect His presence; He will guide you and cause you to grow. God will not let His Word return empty (Isaiah 55:11) as you study it both individually and with the others in the group.

5. But do not expect the Spirit to do your work for you. Start early. Prepare well. As time permits, do additional reading about the topic.

6. Begin and end with prayer.

7. Begin and end on time. Punctuality is a courtesy to everyone and can be a factor that will encourage discussion.

8. Find ways to keep the session informal: Meet in casual surroundings. Arrange seating so participants can face one another. Ask volunteers to provide refreshments.

9. Keep the class moving. Limit your discussion to questions of interest to the participants. Be selective. You don't need to cover every question and every Bible verse.

10. Build one another up through your fellowship and study. You have your needs; other group members have theirs. Together you have a lot to gain.

11. Be sensitive to any participants who may have needs related to the specific problems discussed in this course, especially anyone who may need Christian counseling and professional help.

12. Be a "gatekeeper." That means you may need to shut the gate on one person while you open it for someone else. Involve everyone, especially those who hesitate to speak.

▲ If You Are Using This Study on Your Own

1. Each time you sit down to study a session, ask the Holy Spirit for guidance and counsel. Expect Him to work through His Word to encourage, motivate, and empower you to grow in your faith.

2. Study the Bible texts printed in the course with special care. God works through His Word. In it you will find power. Read each text slowly, several times.

3. Write answers in the spaces provided. Avoid the temptation just "to think" your responses. Writing will force you to be specific. It's in that specificity you are most likely to identify crucial issues for yourself. Check the Leaders Notes in the back of this guide for information you may find helpful as you go along.

4. Pray as you work. Ask God to show you what He wants you to see about Him, about yourself, and about your family situation.

1

A Mother ▼
Is a Daughter

Opening Prayer

Lord, help me to forget all those things that keep
me from spending time with You and the family
You've given me. Lord, help me to remember You are
my Father, I am Your child. Nothing will ever change
that. Help me to see You as my source of strength,
hope, and wisdom. I ask this in my Savior's name.
Amen.

Focusing Our Attention

*I'm not sure what excited me most. My daughter's
first tooth, first step, or her first successful trip to the
potty chair. They were all milestone moments. As soon
as these events occurred, I immediately headed for the
phone to make the long distance call to my mother.
Even though I also shared these special times with
others, it was never quite the same as sharing them
with my mom. Somehow this long distance communication had a way of shortening the distance between
our hearts. As my love and admiration for my daughter grew, the love and admiration I had for my mother
also grew.*

1. With a partner or the members of a small

group, share the following information about your mother or the mother-figure in your life.

- name
- birthplace
- family background
- education
- most memorable quality

2. Discuss the statement "You never really appreciate your parents until you have a child of your own."

Focusing on the Issue

Read the following account about Kathy and her mother.

Kathy is 33. Her widowed mother is 74. Kathy and her mom speak to each other regularly—usually at least twice a week. They talk about the weather, her job, yard work, and the relatives. One topic they never discuss is their love and appreciation for one another.

They often speak face to face, but rarely, if ever, speak heart to heart. Although her mom is in good health, Kathy fears her mom will die before she is ever able to tell her how much she loves her. Kathy has wanted to tell her mother about her love for her for several years now.

Kathy grew up knowing her parents loved her, although she never heard the words "I love you" from either of her parents. Vowing she will be different from her mother, Kathy daily tells her children she loves them. Because she wants them to feel loved, she also refuses to spank or discipline them unless their actions are absolutely intolerable. Her children recognize their power over her and use it often to get new toys, special privileges, and sugary treats. Their constant begging, fighting, and demanding tire and frustrate Kathy. Sometimes she wishes she could simply run away.

Kathy's husband has never agreed with her overly lenient treatment of the children.

Kathy is confused and concerned. She doesn't know where she went wrong. She gave her children the one thing she most wanted from her mother. She'd like to talk to her mother about all of this. She'd like to tell her mother she loves her, but she is desperately afraid her mother will respond with something like, "Why are you saying you love me now? Do you think I'm going to die or something?" She has tried telling herself to just tell her mom she loves her and not worry about how her mom may respond. However, she doesn't think she could handle the pain if her mom does not respond with an "I love you too." So she remains silent.

1. How is Kathy's life as a daughter interfering with her life as a mother?

2. What are some things Kathy can do to change her situation?

3. If Kathy's mother suddenly told her she loved her, would you expect to see a dramatic change in Kathy's parenting? Why or why not?

Focusing on God's Word

1. Consider the following passages. Comment after each on why no one who trusts in Jesus as his or her Savior is ever a spiritual orphan.

a. Though my father and mother forsake me, the LORD will receive me (Psalm 27:10).

b. Sing to God, sing praises to His name, extol Him who rides on the clouds—His name is the LORD—and rejoice before Him. A father to the fatherless, a defender of widows, is God in His holy dwelling. God sets the lonely in families, He leads forth the prisoners with singing; but the rebellious live in a sun-scorched land (Psalm 68:5–6).

c. Shout for joy, O heavens; rejoice, O earth; burst into song, O mountains! For the LORD comforts His people and will have compassion on His afflicted ones ... "Can a mother forget the baby at her breast and have no compassion on the child she has borne? Though she may forget, I will not forget you!" (Isaiah 49:13, 15).

d. As a mother comforts her child, so will I comfort you; and you will be comforted over Jerusalem (Isaiah 66:13).

2. How is God the Father like our earthly fathers and mothers? How is He different from our fathers and mothers?

3. Scripture says, "God sets the lonely in families." How can earthly families keep us from feeling lonely?

4. In his gospel John records, "As the Father has loved Me, so have I loved you" (John 15:9). Jesus loves us with a perfect, complete, and unselfish love. Because He loved us, He willingly suffered and died to take the horrible and eternal punishment for our sins upon Himself. Now, by faith, God has made us His children. As such, we have the power of the Holy Spirit, changing us as we read, study, and reflect upon God's Word.

Read the following passage. Explain the spiritual growth and maturity God desires to bring into the lives of His children.

▼▼▼▼▼▼▼▼▼▼▼▼▼▼▼▼▼▼▼▼▼▼▼▼▼▼▼

For this reason I kneel before the Father, from whom His whole family in heaven and on earth derives its name. I pray that out of His glorious riches He may strengthen you with power through His Spirit in your inner being, so that Christ may dwell in your hearts through faith. And I pray that you, being rooted and established in love, may have power, together with all the saints, to grasp how wide and long and high and deep is the love of Christ, and to know this love that surpasses knowledge—that you may be filled to the measure of all the fullness of God. (Ephesians 3:14–19)

▲▲▲▲▲▲▲▲▲▲▲▲▲▲▲▲▲▲▲▲▲▲▲▲▲▲▲

Focusing on My Life

Read the following thoughts on Christian motherhood.

I wanted to be the perfect Christian mother, but I knew how impatient and selfish I could be at times. I knew I was a sinner. I knew I could not be a perfect mother, but wondered if I could be a good mother. I just did not feel wise enough or strong enough for this all-important once-in-a-lifetime opportunity.

While I certainly did have fears, I also had strength and comfort because I knew I'd always be a daughter—a daughter of One who was all-wise and all-powerful and all-forgiving. As I cradled my child, I remembered the Child who was cradled in the Bethlehem barn and how He died for my sins as well as the sins my child would commit. As I held my young daughter, I knew I, too, was being held by the only perfect parent—God, the Father.

1. Comment on the importance of forgiveness in your relationship with yourself as well as with the others in your family.

2. Think back briefly on your childhood. What were some of the sad times—times when you may have felt lonely, afraid, or rejected, times when your mother or father showed poor judgment or deliberately hurt you? Ask God to help you leave these situations behind you. Pray the following:

Dear Lord, forgive my parents for the mistakes they made. Forgive me also for the sins in my life. Help me to learn from all these mistakes. Let them not interfere with my parenting or take from me the joy of being Your child. Send Your Holy Spirit to guide, direct, and bless my parenting. I pray this in the name of Jesus who lived, died, and rose again for me. Amen.

3. What did your parents do right when it comes to:

Discipline—

Religious training—

Faith sharing—

Making memories—

Holidays—

Encouraging education—

Teaching the value of money—

▼

Sex education—

Teaching responsibility—

Communication—

Giving hugs and kisses—

Rules—

Mealtimes—

Manners—

4. How have your parents affected your parenting? Would you say you are following in their footsteps or blazing a new trail?

5. What do you most want your children to remember about you? What are you doing to give them the memories you want them to have?

To Do at Home

1. Call, write, or speak to your mother or father. Recall with them whatever was true, noble, right, pure, lovely, admirable, excellent, or praiseworthy about your childhood and their parenting.

2. Ask your children to share some of their favorite memories with you. Consider writing them down for future reference. Young children may prefer to draw pictures of their memories. These drawings can be kept in a scrapbook with the written memories.

3. Make a memory. Go to a special place, play a favorite game, do one of those things you always say you are going to do someday with your family.

Closing Prayer

Join together as a group for this closing prayer. Choose one person to read the Leader sections while all other participants respond with the Response sections.

Leader: Lord, You have given me many yesterdays and I thank You for each of them.

Response: You have given me only one today. Help me to use it for the good of my family and for Your glory.

Leader: Grant me wisdom and patience.

Response: Help me to deal with my children the way You deal with Your children.

Leader: Draw each of us ever closer to each other, our families, and most of all, draw us ever closer to You.

Response: For You are our Father in heaven, hallowed be Your name, Your kingdom come, Your will be done on earth as in heaven. Give us today our daily bread. Forgive us our sins as we forgive those who sin against us. Lead us not into temptation, but deliver us from evil. For the kingdom, the power, and the glory are Yours now and forever. Amen.

A Mother Is a Mother

2

Opening Prayer

Lord, teach us how to be the kind of parents You want us to be. Open us to the guidance of Your Word. Draw us closer to You as we learn from You. Thank You for being our all-wise Father while we struggle to become wiser parents. We pray in Jesus' name. Amen.

Focusing Our Attention

With a partner or with two or three others in a small group, share the following:
* where you grew up
* a favorite family activity from your childhood
* a completion to this sentence: When I was a child, my mother made the best:

Focusing on the Issue

Read the following account about a mother named Rhonda.

When Rhonda was a child, she seldom brought friends to her home. She felt uneasy about her home's usually messy—sometimes dirty—appearance. Her mom worked hard on the family's farm and seldom had time or energy left to care for the house or even herself. Rhonda remembers cringing when her mom picked her up at school with uncombed hair, wearing torn, unmatched or slightly dirty clothes.

As an adult with a home of her own, Rhonda always made the appearance of her home a priority and enjoyed having her children's friends around the house. She was quick to join their conversations, used all the latest slang expressions, played their kind of music, and even showed the girls how to dance. She always volunteered to take them shopping or out for a movie and pizza.

At one point most of her daughter's friends called her "mom." Rhonda did not mind at first, but, after a while, she asked them to just call her Rhonda. She liked that better because it made her feel more like one of them. Eventually, she became so popular with this group of fourteen-year-old girls that sometimes one of them would call just to talk to her.

One Saturday morning, Rhonda chattered eagerly about all the fun they had had shopping the night before when she noticed a tear trickling from her daughter Lindsay's eye. When Rhonda asked what was wrong, her daughter responded with the usual, "Nothing." After pleading with her to tell what was wrong, her daughter finally said, "Mom, it's just that sometimes I wonder who my friends like most—me or you. I wonder if they'd still ask me to go places or do things with them if you weren't always right there to take us places and buy us pizza. I'm glad you spend time with us. I'm glad you like my friends and I'm really proud of you, but most of all, I just want you to be my mom."

1. Do you think Rhonda has a good relationship with her daughter? Why or why not?

2. How are the roles of friend and mother similar? How are they different?

3. Should Rhonda change her behavior? If so, how and why?

4. Chances are you made some statements about motherhood while you were still a child. Recall some of the ways you may have completed the statement, "When I'm a parent, I'm never going to ..." or "When I'm the parent, I will always ...."

5. How many, if any, of these idealistic vows have you kept? Would it have been good to keep all of them? Why or why not?

6. God gives parents authority over their children. God also gives others authority over us and over our children. Sometimes it is very easy to forget the awesome responsibility of being and upholding authorities in the lives of our children. We are afraid we will separate ourselves from our children, incur their wrath, or lose their love if we do this. In reality, when we fail to exert ourselves as parents, we may be giving our children permission to sin and cause them to lose respect for other authorities. Consider the following comments made by parents and the possible consequences of their words. What attitudes are they instilling and how will these attitudes affect their relationships with their children?

19
▼

a. "I don't mind if you have your friends over for a party. I'll even buy the beer, but I'm collecting the keys. No one leaves here unless I think they are sober enough to drive home."

b. "I'll be happy if you even pass that test with a 'D.' That teacher is so unfair. I remember having teachers like that. They make you feel like you don't even want to study. Don't worry about it."

c. "I hope you aren't having sex—especially with multiple partners. But if you are, I want you to be protected. If you have any questions about condoms or need money for them, let me know."

d. "No bus driver is going to talk to my child that way! I'll call her supervisor in the morning. Maybe she'll understand what it feels like to be threatened about losing riding privileges when she is threatened losing driving privileges. Don't worry about it. That's what you have a mother for."

All parents fail at times. Fortunately, our heavenly Father is ready to forgive our every sin and to guide, strengthen, and renew us for Jesus' sake. He and He alone is the Perfect Parent.

Focusing on a Mother's Role

Some 2,000 years ago the Maker and Ruler of the universe sent His only Son to become a tiny baby. Born to a young woman named Mary, Jesus grew to live a perfect life and to die a painful death to pay for the sins of all people. Just as God planned for Mary to love and care for the Savior of the world, born to her as a little boy, God has especially designed women for the great privilege of bringing children into the world to love them and teach them about love during the most important, formative years of their lives.

Comment on each of the following quotes about the uniqueness of motherhood.

1. From God's Holy Word.

a. I have been reminded of your sincere faith, which first lived in your grandmother Lois and in your mother Eunice and, I am persuaded, now lives in you also.... But as for you, continue in what you have learned and have become convinced of, because you know those from whom you learned it, and how from infancy you have known the holy Scriptures, which are able to make you wise for salvation through faith in Christ Jesus (2 Timothy 1:5, 3:14–15).

b. After he was weaned, she took the boy with her, young as he was, along with a three-year-old bull, an ephah of flour and a skin of wine, and brought him to the house of the LORD at Shiloh. When they had slaughtered the bull, they brought the boy to Eli, and she said to him, "As surely as you live, my lord, I am the woman who stood here beside you praying to the

LORD. I prayed for this child, and the LORD has granted me what I asked of Him. So now I give him to the LORD. For his whole life he will be given over to the LORD." And he worshiped the LORD there (1 Samuel 1:24–28).

c. She is clothed with strength and dignity; she can laugh at the days to come. She speaks with wisdom, and faithful instruction is on her tongue. She watches over the affairs of her household and does not eat the bread of idleness. Her children arise and call her blessed; her husband also, and he praises her: "Many women do noble things, but you surpass them all." Charm is deceptive, and beauty is fleeting; but a woman who fears the LORD is to be praised (Proverbs 31:25–30).

2. From history and tradition.
a. A four-year-old boy once told a young friend, "Mom is at a meeting, so Dad and Billy and Amy and Carrie and Justin and Ruthie and I are home all alone."

b. An ounce of mother is worth a pound of clergy.
—Spanish Proverb

c. Martin Luther has been credited with the following statement, "When Eve was brought to Adam, he gave her the most glorious of appellations. He called her Eve, that is to say, the Mother of All. He did not style her wife, but simply mother. In this consists the glory and the most precious ornament of woman."

d. A child without a mother is like a door without a knob. —Jewish Proverb

To Do at Home

1. Write a diary or journal entry entitled, "I'm glad I'm a mother because ..."

2. Visit your local library or bookstore. Read a book or article about parenting—possibly even a humorous one.

3. Ask your children to describe the ideal mom. Talk to them about what they most enjoy doing with you. If your children are very young, ask them to draw a picture of themselves doing something special with you. Put it on the refrigerator as a happy reminder to spend time with each other.

4. Make a list of your goals as a parent. Place them in your Bible. Look at them from time to time. Ask God for the strength to accomplish these goals if they are His goals for you.

Closing Prayer

Pray the following. Invite those on the left side of the room to read the Leader sections and those on the right to respond with the Response sections.

Leader: Lord, when You were here on earth, You were the perfect Child. But, like me, Lord, my children are not perfect. Children sometimes think they are, but they aren't.

Response: Father, forgive us. Help us to look for the good in all people. Forgive us, Lord, for the sake of Your Son, our Savior, who shed His blood for us.

Leader: Sometimes my children are so disorganized. They need to be reminded of their chores. I get so frustrated I could scream, and too often I do just that.

Response: Lord, often my life isn't perfectly organized either and I, too, forget to do what You have asked me to do. I ignore Your commands. Forgive me, Lord. Forgive my impatience. Help me to appreciate and enjoy all the members of my family.

All: Lord, You are the only Perfect One in our family. Thank You for always loving, accepting, and forgiving us. Teach us how to be loving, accepting, and forgiving of others. Most of all thank You for being our Father in heaven, hallowed be Your name, Your kingdom come, Your will be done on earth as in heaven. Give us today our daily bread. Forgive us our sins as we forgive those who sin against us. Lead us not into temptation, but deliver us from evil. For the kingdom, the power, and the glory are Yours now and forever. Amen.

3

A Mother Is Forgiven and Forgiving

Opening Prayer

Lord, when I see the sins of others, point me to Your cross. Give me a desire to continue to forgive all people, instead of sinning against them in order to give them what I feel they deserve. You suffered the pain You did not deserve so I could be forgiven. Help me to accept the forgiveness You paid the ultimate price to earn. Sin always hurts. Forgiveness strengthens and heals. Teach me how to forgive others the way You have forgiven me. In Jesus' name. Amen.

Focusing Our Attention

Focus on one of the following family activities and share with a partner or with three or four others in a small group about a particular outing you enjoyed with your family.

- going to the zoo
- hiking in the mountains
- camping
- floating down the river
- visiting relatives
- spending the day at the amusement park
- picnicking

Focusing Our Sights

Consider the following true story about forgiveness.

My second-grade daughter had learned to do some basic multiplying. Fascinated and impressed, I was giving her a final good night kiss, when I noticed the problem 70×7 written on a scrap of notebook paper. With evidence of much trial and a few initial errors, she had determined the correct answer—490. I noticed the same number appeared at the top of a second sheet of otherwise blank paper.

I did not see that paper again for about a week. Then I noticed some tick marks carefully grouped in neat, easily-countable bundles of five. Gradually, it became clear what my daughter was doing. Each tick mark indicated an occasion when she felt she had forgiven her younger brother for one of his many sins against her. Remembering the passage she had memorized only a few short weeks ago, she had very literally interpreted the King James Version of Matthew 18:21–22, which reads, "Then came Peter to Him, and said, Lord, how oft shall my brother sin against me, and I forgive him? till seven times? Jesus saith unto him, 'I say not unto thee, Until seven times: but, Until seventy times seven.' "

She was ready and waiting for number 491.

1. Is forgetting a part of forgiving? If it is, what can we do to help the forgetting process even if we can still remember the event?

2. How do mothers sometimes behave like this little girl when it comes to the sins of their children?

3. Explain the meaning of Matthew 18:21–22. How often should we forgive someone—especially for the same sin?

Focusing on the Issue

Read the following.

That one-of-a-kind collector's plate was probably worth $100. I had hung it up so that others could enjoy its beauty. The more I looked at the broken pieces, the more I felt somebody had to pay—not with money, but with suffering. I hadn't broken the plate so why should I suffer?

Billy had broken the plate. He should suffer. He should know how angry he had made me—how hurt I felt. I had had a long hard day and now to come home to this. I marched into Billy's room and found him asleep on his bed. That only angered me more. I called his name and gently rocked his shoulders. His father assured me that he had been scolded, but I didn't care. I wanted him to know how much he had hurt me. I called his name and rocked his shoulders again.

This time two sad eyes opened half way as a puckering mouth uttered the unforgettable words, "I'm sorry." Suddenly his arms found my arms and we ended up hugging and holding each other as I said my two word sermon. "You're forgiven."

As I nestled my almost-seven-year-old son in my lap, my heart raced with joy—the unexplainable joy of forgiveness. As I quietly reflected on the events of the evening, I thought about how often I too had hurt God and others through my actions. Yet when God looks at His Son and hears my quivering, "I'm sorry"—His strong arms lift me into His lap of love and I experience the joy of His total forgiveness. I thought about my son and His Son. I thanked God for both of them.

The plate is forever broken. His promise, "Since we have been justified through faith, we have peace with God through our Lord Jesus Christ" (Romans 5:1) will never be broken.

1. Why is it important for adults as well as children to say, "I'm sorry"?

2. How did this mother and son help each other to feel forgiven? What ways can you help your children to feel forgiven?

Focusing on God's Word

1. Luke 23:34 records Jesus, during His crucifixion, asking His heavenly Father to forgive the people who were crucifying Him. While suffering excruciating pain He prayed, "Father, forgive them, for they do not know what they are doing." As far as we know, no one at the foot of the cross had asked for forgiveness. How can we learn from His example? What practical application does this have for each of us within our families?

2. According to the following, why is forgiveness not optional for God's people? How does this attitude toward forgiveness differ from the advice we might receive from worldly sources?

For if you forgive men when they sin against you, your heavenly Father will also forgive you. But if you do not forgive men their sins, your Father will not forgive your sins (Matthew 6:14–15).

3. As you read the following verses, think about the role of forgiveness in the life of a believer.

"Therefore, as God's chosen people, holy and dearly loved, clothe yourselves with compassion, kindness, humility, gentleness and patience. Bear with each other and forgive whatever grievances you may have against one another. Forgive as the Lord forgave you" (Colossians 3:12–13).

"Do not let any unwholesome talk come out of your mouths, but only what is helpful for building others up according to their needs, that it may benefit those who listen. And do not grieve the Holy Spirit of God, with whom you were sealed for the day of redemption. Get rid of all bitterness, rage and anger, brawling and slander, along with every form of malice. Be kind and compassionate to one another, forgiving each other, just as in Christ God forgave you" (Ephesians 4:29–32).

a. In each passage of the preceding passages, what is pointed out as the reason for forgiving?

b. Recognizing how one sin can lead to another sin (saying things we should not say can lead to anger, bitterness, and slander), how can one act of forgiveness lead to another?

Focusing on My Life

Complete the following survey to help you think about the role of forgiveness in your life.

1. Whom do you find most difficult to forgive?

_____ family members

_____ close friends

_____ casual acquaintances

_____ estranged friends

_____ business associates

_____ yourself

2. When do you find it most difficult to forgive? Check as many as apply.

_____ when a person does not ask for forgiveness

_____ when it is not the first time the person has committed this sin against you

_____ when someone hurts you physically

_____ when someone hurts you emotionally

_____ when someone has hurt a person you love

_____ when much time has gone by since the offense

_____ immediately after the offense

_____ when someone gossips or spreads rumors about you or a family member but is pleasant when they are in contact with you

_____ when you have not been faithful in prayer and Bible study

_____ when someone refuses to forgive you

_____ when you are already bitter because you have not totally forgiven another person

3. When or where do you feel most forgiven?

_____ after communing

_____ in church

_____ after someone has told you you're forgiven for a specific offense

_____ after praying privately

_____ other time and/or place:

4. What have you learned about yourself from this informal survey?

5. What, if anything, would you most like God's help in changing when it comes to your forgiving? How could making these changes improve your parenting?

To Do at Home

1. Consciously use the words "You're forgiven" when family members and others say they are sorry.

2. Make a poster, mini banner, or refrigerator magnet showing the math problem 70 × 7. Display it as a visual reminder of the unlimited forgiveness God freely enables us to extend to one another.

3. Be quick to say "I'm sorry" to your family whenever you need to confess a sin. Rather than a sign of

your weakness, saying "I'm sorry" evidences His strength within you.

4. Write a letter or make a phone call or personal visit to anyone you may need to forgive.

Closing Prayer

Join together as a group for this closing prayer. Again choose one person to read the Leader sections while all other participants respond with the Response sections.

Leader: Lord, You and You alone know some of those half-forgiven and unforgiven situations in my life.

Response: By Your power, I now forgive these sins as You forgive me.

Leader: Lord, help my children and husband to forgive me for all the times I hurt them knowingly or unknowingly.

Response: By Your power, bring us closer together, never again to be separated by unforgiven sin.

All: Our Father in heaven, hallowed be Your name, Your kingdom come, Your will be done on earth as in heaven. Give us today our daily bread. Forgive us our sins as we forgive those who sin against us. Lead us not into temptation, but deliver us from evil. For the kingdom, the power, and the glory are Yours now and forever. Amen.

A Mother Is Loved and Loving

4

Opening Prayer

Lord, Your Word tells us "God is love." We thank and praise You for Your great unending love for us—a love that moved You to send Your only Son to live, die, and rise again for us. Help us to know and understand You better. For if we do not know You, we cannot know love. Help us to love You and others with the ability to love that only Your Spirit can give. We pray in Jesus' name. Amen.

Focusing Our Attention

Following is a list of ways parents show love for their children. Reflecting on a parent's love for you, which of the these ways best describes the evidence of that love you remember most? Share your response with a partner or with two or three others in a small group.

- verbalizing
- believing
- protecting
- encouraging
- giving
- sacrificing
- enduring

- hoping
- sharing
- hugging

Focusing on the Issue

She could have bought it in the store, but she didn't. One way or another Marilyn was going to finish this costume for her son, Jimmy. Sewing costumes is simply the kind of thing a mother should do, Marilyn thought. She couldn't wait to see Jimmy in it at the school play—saying his lines and acting with the other kids. "If only I could sew," Marilyn moaned quietly to herself as she stuffed more pins into her mouth and straightened the fabric to feed it into the sewing machine.

Jimmy frequently entered the room to check on the progress. "Love you, Mom," he would say. "Can I see my costume now?"

After several such encounters with the excited and eager Jimmy, a frustrated Marilyn replied, "I love you, too, Jimmy; but I'd love you even more if you'd just leave me alone for a little while."

Then Jimmy left and Marilyn suddenly began to cry.

1. Are you able to identify with the feelings of this mother? If so, which ones?

2. Thinking about your particular role as a mother, finish these statements:

It is easy for me to love my child(ren) when

Focusing on God's Word

God's love for us led Him to act on our behalf despite our lack of lovable qualities. Romans 5:8 records, "But God demonstrates His own love for us in this: While we were still sinners, Christ died for us." His life, death, and resurrection evidence His unconditional love. As the result of the ultimate sacrifice He gave for us, by faith we receive the forgiveness, salvation, and renewed spiritual strength He has won for us and all people.

As the love of Christ reaches us and changes us, by faith His Spirit continues to change us, causing to emerge within us the increasing desire and ability to love others unconditionally and continuously, just as God loves us. Love is a reflex, a natural inclination, but at times love involves making a decision to act in a loving way, even when we don't feel like it.

1. Although the love of a mother for her child is among the most unselfish of affections, mothers, too, sometimes fail in their desire to speak and act lovingly toward their children. Consider each of the following verses. Write a phrase or sentence applying each verse to the challenges and failures of an imperfect yet loving mother.

a. Love covers over a multitude of sins (1 Peter 4:8).

b. This is how God showed His love among us: He sent His one and only Son into the world that we might live through Him. This is love: not that we loved God, but that He loved us and sent His Son as an atoning sacrifice for our sins. Dear friends, since God so loved us, we also ought to love one another. No one has ever seen God; but if we love one another, God lives in us and His love is made complete in us (1 John 4:9–12).

c. I said, "I will confess my transgressions to the LORD"—and You forgave the guilt of my sin (Psalm 32:5).

d. Dear children, let us not love with words or tongue but with actions and in truth. This then is how we know that we belong to the truth, and how we set our hearts at rest in His presence whenever our hearts condemn us. For God is greater than our hearts, and He knows everything. Dear friends, if our hearts do not condemn us, we have confidence before God and receive from Him anything we ask, because we obey His commands and do what pleases Him (1 John 3:18–22).

2. Read the following verses to reflect upon the perfect love God has for us—the love that motivates us in our relationships with others including those

closest to us. Fill in the chart to identify what true love is and isn't.

▼▼▼▼▼▼▼▼▼▼▼▼▼▼▼▼▼▼▼▼▼▼▼▼▼▼

If I speak in the tongues of men and of angels, but have not love, I am only a resounding gong or a clanging cymbal. If I have the gift of prophecy and can fathom all mysteries and all knowledge, and if I have a faith that can move mountains, but have not love, I am nothing. If I give all I possess to the poor and surrender my body to the flames, but have not love, I gain nothing.

Love is patient, love is kind. It does not envy, it does not boast, it is not proud. It is not rude, it is not self-seeking, it is not easily angered, it keeps no record of wrongs. Love does not delight in evil but rejoices with the truth. It always protects, always trusts, always hopes, always perseveres. Love never fails. (1 Corinthians 13:1–8a)

▲▲▲▲▲▲▲▲▲▲▲▲▲▲▲▲▲▲▲▲▲▲▲▲▲

LOVE IS ...   LOVE ISN'T ...

3. While it is most important for families to find and share God's love within the home, it is also important for children to love and feel loved by people who are not immediate household members. How can you apply the following passage to your family life?

▼▼▼▼▼▼▼▼▼▼▼▼▼▼▼▼▼▼▼▼▼▼▼▼▼▼

Love must be sincere. Hate what is evil; cling to what is good. Be devoted to one another in brotherly love. Honor one another above yourselves. Never be lacking in zeal, but keep your spiritual fervor, serving the Lord. Be joyful in hope, patient in affliction, faithful in prayer. Share with God's people who are in need. Practice hospitality. (Romans 12:9–13)

▲▲▲▲▲▲▲▲▲▲▲▲▲▲▲▲▲▲▲▲▲▲▲▲▲▲

Love in Action

Remember how you cuddled your very young child and assured him or her of your love before he or she was even able to speak. Recall how much love you felt the first time your son or daughter snuggled in your arms or grasped you tightly around the neck and proclaimed, "I missed you!" Whether that memory is as fresh as today or is a blur from many years ago, it remains a part of both of your lives.

As our children grow and change, our ways of receiving and communicating love also change. The lap sitting becomes time set aside for sharing the joys and sorrows of the day. Time spent praying together may have changed to time spent praying for one another. Pats on the shoulder replace wrestling on the floor. Letters and boxes of cookies sent to college replace the little love notes once sent in a school lunch bag ... but always there is love and always there must be an expression of it.

1. Share with the group a unique way your family has for sharing love. For example, one mother

remembers quieting her children in church by holding their hands and squeezing three times. These three squeezes meant "I love you." The children responded to this signal by squeezing her hand twice. These two squeezes meant "How much?" She would then squeeze their hand tightly to show them how much she loved them. Usually the children would then respond by squeezing her hand three times to say "I love you" to her and the game would continue.

2. As God works in our lives through His Word, He makes us more loving. Consider the following quote by Donald Grey Barnhouse. Then add one or more statements of your own following a similar pattern.

Joy is love singing.
Peace is love resting.
Long-suffering is love enduring.
Kindness is love's touch.
Goodness is love's character.
Faithfulness is love's habit.
Gentleness is love's self-forgetfulness.
Self-control is love holding the reins.

3. React to the statement, "Sometimes love means holding the line."

▼

4. Think back over the past week. How did you personally and openly show your love to members of your family? Think about actual words you spoke or specific deeds you did. Write a few in the space provided.

5. Think back over your week. How did members of your family show their love for you? Think about their actual words spoken and deeds done. Did you feel loved and accepted? If so, what could you do to thank them? If you did not feel loved, what could you do to convey to them your need for their love?

To Do at Home

1. Write a love note to each member of your immediate family. Send the notes in the mail so they arrive as a surprise.

2. As a family, befriend a person who might be lonely. Visit or invite him or her into your home.

3. Bake a heart-shaped cake. Make a special meal. Set the table with your best dishes. Treat your family as you treat your friends, and your friends as your family. Treat your family as though they were the most special people who have ever entered your home because they are. Celebrate the love you have for one another.

Closing Prayer

Join together to pray the following litany. Ask one person to read the Leader section. All other members of the group respond with the Response sections.

Leader: Lord, there are those days and those times when I do not feel loved, even within my own family. Often this causes me to treat my family in unloving ways. I say things I shouldn't. I don't say the things I should. Before long, we are all running short on love and patience.

Response: Forgive me, Lord. Fill me with Your love. Give me the desire to be loving even when others are not. Remind me daily of Your love for me.

Leader: Lord, thank You for sending Your own Son into our world to die for our sins.

Response: We cannot begin to understand Your love for us, but help us to be imitators of that love. Use our families to spread Your love to all people.

All: Our Father in heaven, hallowed be Your name, Your kingdom come, Your will be done on earth as in heaven. Give us today our daily bread. Forgive us our sins as we forgive those who sin against us. Lead us not into temptation, but deliver us from evil. For the Kingdom, the power, and the glory are Yours now and forever. Amen.

5

A Mother Teaches and Is Taught

Opening Prayer

Lord, teach us what You would have us teach our children. Grant us wisdom, knowledge, and understanding. Guide us and direct us. Open our hearts and minds to Your Word, Your ways, and our children's needs. In Your name we pray. Amen.

Focusing Our Attention

Armed with my calculator, I was hot on the trail of a $2.29 checkbook error, while my five-year-old was working on a stack of worksheets she had found in a reading kit. Whenever she completed one, she brought it to me for correction. Time and again I corrected her papers finding no errors. On the sixth sheet, I finally spotted an error. I marked it wrong and handed it back to her.

She brought it back and wanted to know what was wrong. Annoyed by yet another interruption, I looked at the worksheet with her. It pictured a piece of ice and underneath the picture the child could mark either "cold or not cold." It also featured a ball and the choices were "round or not round." She had every item correct except for one—a picture of a girl sitting on a rock in a field all by herself. The correct response was "alone." She had marked "not alone." Impatiently, I showed her the picture and explained the correct answer was "alone" since there was no one in the field with her. With the unshakable conviction of a child, she stated, "But Mom, she's not alone. God is with her."

Suddenly the one who was correcting had been corrected. The one who was teaching had been taught.

Share with a partner or with the others in a group of three or four about a time when you learned a lesson from a child.

Focusing on the Issue

When our children are very young, we teach them how to tie their shoes, how to conduct themselves in a mannerly way, and how to ride bikes. As time goes on, we teach them how to deal with difficulties with friends and authority figures in their lives. We attempt to teach them life skills as well. Before we release them to begin making their own way in the world, we equip them to manage money, cook nutritious meals, do their laundry, and to perform simple repair and maintenance procedures.

We teach deliberately by telling and demonstrating. But we also teach informally through our everyday actions, attitudes, decisions, and priorities. Unfortunately, we don't always teach things we want our children to learn. What are each of the following parents teaching their children?

1. Reacting to the difficulties and tragedies of her life, Maggie makes the protection of the children her number one priority. She constantly cautions her children about potential dangers and hazards.

2. Betty and her husband, Mike, attend church regularly and pray with and for their children.

3. In an attempt to raise positive children, Wilma never willingly allows her children to see her frustrated, angry, or hurt.

4. Jan and Joe talk with their children about God and His love, weaving their relationship with Jesus into every aspect of their lives.

5. Polly encourages her children to talk with her about everything—especially about their feelings. She regularly asks them for forgiveness when she has been wrong.

The Most Important Thing to Learn

Read the following interchange between a mother and her adult daughter. Then continue with the questions that follow.

"I'm sorry, Valerie," said the elderly woman to her

adult daughter. "I brought you into such a hard world. I know your life hasn't been easy."

"Ah, Mom," replied Valerie, "my life has been good. And I have much to be thankful for. When I was a little girl, you taught me that because we have Jesus as our Savior and each other as a family, we are rich. All the time I was growing up, I believed those words because you said them. Now I believe them because I know they are true; I have seen it for myself."

1. These words between mother and daughter echo the following verse from Paul's second epistle to the Corinthians: "For you know the grace of our Lord Jesus Christ, that though He was rich, yet for your sakes He became poor, so that you through His poverty might become rich" (2 Corinthians 8:9). What riches are possessed by those who believe in Jesus' life, death, and resurrection for them?

2. All who trust in Jesus as their Savior have a new life to live—one that began when we came to faith and extends into eternity. Christian parents have the privilege and obligation of encouraging their children along the way by teaching them about God in their conversations, in their daily lives, and in their use of Word and Sacrament—the means of grace through which the Holy Spirit works the saving faith. Consider the following verses from God's Word. Comment on the message of each for parents concerned about the Christian nurture of their children.

a. These commandments that I give you today are to be upon your hearts. Impress them on your children. Talk about them when you sit at home and when you walk along the road, when you lie down and when you get up. Tie them as symbols on your hands and bind them on your foreheads. Write them on the doorframes of your houses and on your gates (Deuteronomy 6:6–9).

b. Teach me, O LORD, to follow Your decrees; then I will keep them to the end. Give me understanding, and I will keep Your law and obey it with all my heart. Direct me in the path of Your commands, for there I find delight. Turn my heart toward Your statutes and not toward selfish gain. Turn my eyes from worthless things; preserve my life according to Your word (Psalm 119:33–37).

c. Teach me to do Your will, for You are my God; may Your good Spirit lead me on level ground (Psalm 143:10).

d. All Scripture is God-breathed and is useful for teaching, rebuking, correcting and training in right-eousness, so that the man of God may be thoroughly equipped for every good work (2 Timothy 3:16–17).

e. For the grace of God that brings salvation has appeared to all men. It teaches us to say "No" to ungodliness and worldly passions, and to live self-controlled, upright and godly lives in this present age, while we wait for the blessed hope—the glorious appearing of our great God and Savior, Jesus Christ, who gave Himself for us to redeem us from all wickedness and to purify for Himself a people that are His very own, eager to do what is good (Titus 2:11–14).

3. From Naomi to Ruth to Obed to Jesse to David, from his grandmother Lois to his mother Eunice to Timothy, from generation to generation, the people of God bring the saving faith to the generations that follow them. The transmission of faith happens only by the working of the Holy Spirit through God's Word. Consider each of the following teachable moments from the life of a young person. With a partner or with others in a group of two or three, discuss the opportunity each offers to teach, model, and otherwise impart the saving faith to the new generation.

a. Fifteen-year-old Jim walks into the kitchen as you are doing the dishes and sits down. Gradually, he reveals to you the reason for his gloomy mood. A friend from school died the night before in an auto accident.

▼

b. You are helping your fifth grade daughter with her science homework. The questions deal with the origin of the universe and the theory of evolution.

c. Your six-year-old son complains about having to go to Sunday school.

d. Your eleven-year-old daughter asks you why some men and women get married and live together while others just live together without being married.

e. You hear the sound of shattering glass. You are angry at your son for deliberately disobeying your rule about playing ball next to the house.

Focusing on My Life

1. Think about your life. Who are the people who have been the most influential in teaching you about God? Check as many as apply.

____ father
____ mother
____ siblings
____ grandparents or other relatives
____ pastor
____ TV evangelist
____ teachers
____ authors of Christian books
____ friends
____ neighbors
____ business or professional contacts
____ Sunday school teacher(s)

2. What did these people do to impact positively your spiritual life? Do you seek to have this type of impact on others? If so, how?

3. If we are to teach His Word and His ways to our children, we must also continue to grow in His Word and His ways. What are you presently doing to facilitate your personal spiritual growth? What are you planning to do in the future?

To Do at Home

1. Ask each of your children if there is something they would like you to teach them. Spend time together learning a new skill or activity—anything from pounding a nail, sewing on a button, or making a favorite cookie recipe. While doing the task, talk to your children about some things you remember learning from your parents. Be sure to share any joy or difficulty you may have had while learning with them.

2. Depending on age levels, teach your children a new song, rhyme, finger play or Bible passage. Share with them what your favorite passages or songs may have been as a child and why. Share your present favorites also.

3. Allow your children to teach you a favorite song or finger play they may have learned at school or Sunday school.

4. Make a commitment to personally memorize a Bible passage each week. Print it on a 3" × 5" card. Tape it to a mirror or near a doorway. Repeat it whenever you see it. Consider reciting it to one of your children when you feel you have mastered it.

Closing Prayer

Join together to pray. One individual or side of the room may read the Leader sections, all others will respond with the Response sections.

Leader: Lord, it has been good to take this time to learn about You, Your Word, and Your will for my family's life. It has helped me think again about what really is important, and what really is not as important as it may sometimes seem.

Response: Give me courage, strength, and

wisdom as I now go forth to share with my family the important truths I have learned. Help me share Your love with my family. Work in our hearts so that we may draw them closer to You and to one another.

Leader: Lord, when You walked on our earth, You taught Your disciples to pray. They taught it to others and others taught it to us.

Response: As Your disciples today, we still pray this prayer.

All: Our Father in heaven, hallowed be Your name, Your kingdom come, Your will be done on earth as in heaven. Give us today our daily bread. Forgive us our sins as we forgive those who sin against us. Lead us not into temptation, but deliver us from evil. For the kingdom, the power, and the glory are Yours now and forever. Amen.

▼

6

A Mother Prays and Is Prayed For

Opening Prayer

Lord, prayer is an opportunity for us to speak to You, to pour out our hearts to You, and to ask You to fill those hearts with Your love and Your hope. You are always more willing to listen than we are to speak. Change that about us, Lord. Fill us with an eagerness to share all of our thoughts and hopes and dreams with You, our Father. We pray in Jesus' name. Amen.

Focusing Our Attention

From among the following methods of communication, choose the ones through which you have received the most valuable information during the past 24 hours. Explain your choice to a partner or to two or three others in a small group.

- newspaper
- letter
- telephone
- radio
- person-to-person conversation
- television
- computer

Focusing on the Issue

Have you ever felt so low, so lonely, that you knew the only one who could possibly care about you or understand you was God? Maybe you even tried to pray, but the words just wouldn't come. Maybe that was the day the teacher called again to tell you about your son's behavior. Maybe it was the day you found pills in your daughter's jacket, or the day you lost your job. Maybe it was the day the doctor found the cancer, or the day you looked at the laundry, the dishes, the uncleaned stove top, and the green fuzzy stuff growing on the last two slices of bread in the house.

All of us have known days when we fail and when we feel like failures. But each of us has a friend to talk to and share with—someone who cares. He cared enough to send His only Son to live a perfect life and die a willing death to pay the penalty for all the wrong things we have done. After His resurrection He promised always to remain with us and to comfort us with His Holy Spirit.

One of the most comforting passages in all of Scripture, Romans 8:26–27, says, "In the same way, the Spirit helps us in our weakness. We do not know what we ought to pray for, but the Spirit Himself intercedes for us with groans that words cannot express. And He who searches our hearts knows the mind of the Spirit, because the Spirit intercedes for the saints in accordance with God's will."

What a comfort! During those times when we are so bewildered and confused that we do not even know what to pray—God knows! Not only does He know exactly what we need, He also intercedes for us. We do not even have to ask Him to pray on our behalf, so great is His love and understanding of us.

Further, we know that just as the Spirit intercedes for us, He also intercedes for our children. Even

53
▼

when we forget to pray for ourselves or our children, He continues to pray for us.

1. At this very moment, God's Holy Spirit is interceding for you. What do you think He might be praying about?

2. When I pray for my children, I am most likely to:

_____ give God thanks for them

_____ ask God to help them with a physical problem

_____ ask God for spiritual blessings for them

_____ ask God for wisdom and patience in dealing with them

3. Consider the following section from Psalm 17, a psalm of David.

I call on you, O God, for You will answer me; give ear to me and hear my prayer. Show the wonder of Your great love, You who save by Your right hand those who take refuge in You from their foes. Keep me as the apple of Your eye; hide me in the shadow of Your wings from the wicked who assail me, from my mortal enemies who surround me. (Psalm 17:6–9)

a. In the words of the preceding verse, why does David, the author, call on God? What does David ask for?

b. What part of the Psalm 17 passage might a mother pray on behalf of her children? Rewrite those words from a mother's perspective.

4. The following words were first prayed by Hannah.

▼▼▼▼▼▼▼▼▼▼▼▼▼▼▼▼▼▼▼▼▼▼▼▼▼▼▼

I prayed for this child, and the LORD has granted me what I asked of Him. So now I give him to the LORD. For his whole life he will be given over to the LORD. (1 Samuel 1:27–28)

▲▲▲▲▲▲▲▲▲▲▲▲▲▲▲▲▲▲▲▲▲▲▲▲▲▲▲

Hannah had waited many years for a child. When God finally gave Hannah her heart's desire, she gave Samuel back to God with this prayer. What aspects of this prayer apply to all who desire to honor God in their motherhood?

5. God, our loving heavenly Father, invites us to come to Him in prayer, confident in the forgiveness we have in Him through Christ. He promises that the love and care He provides us exceeds that of the most loving and caring of parents. According to the following passages, what are the benefits God provides His children through prayer?

a. I tell you the truth, My Father will give you whatever you ask in My name.... Ask and you will receive, and your joy will be complete (John 16:23–24).

b. This is the confidence we have in approaching God: that if we ask anything according to His will, He hears us. And if we know that He hears us—whatever we ask—we know that we have what we asked of Him (1 John 5:14–15).

c. Do not be anxious about anything, but in everything, by prayer and petition, with thanksgiving, present your requests to God. And the peace of God, which transcends all understanding, will guard your hearts and minds in Christ Jesus (Philippians 4:6–7).

d. For where two or three come together in My name, there am I with them (Matthew 18:20).

Focusing on My Life

When God gave us children, He presented us with a great privilege. But He promises us that we don't need to shoulder our parenting alone. As God invites us to talk to Him in prayer, He assures us of His continued peace, presence, and power as His Holy Spirit strengthens us through Word and Sacrament.

In light of God's love for us and the help He offers, how would you explain each of the following?

1. "If charity begins in the home, so also do nurture, stewardship, evangelism, service, fellowship, and worship."

2. "God wanted every young child to feel the touch of love, so He made mothers."

3. "I used to spend time talking to my son about God; now I spend more of my time talking to God about my son."

4. "You didn't have to teach me how to pray, Mom. I heard you pray, I watched you pray, and finally I joined you in prayer."

5. "We join together in prayer to talk to God, but God comes to us in our prayertime, bringing us close to Him and to one another."

The Importance of Communication

Because God loves us, He invites us to communicate with Him regularly and continually. In addition to praying before and after meals, many families set aside a special time each day to meditate briefly upon God's Word and to bring before Him prayers of praise and thanksgiving and petitions for themselves and for others.

1. Which of the following times does (or may) your family set aside for this purpose?

_____immediately upon waking up at a designated time each morning

_____while riding in the car on the way to or from school and work

_____before eating the evening meal

_____after the evening meal

_____before going to bed

2. Reflecting upon your personal prayer life, at which of the following times do you communicate with God?

_____ at meals

_____ at bedtime

_____ in the morning

_____ when you are facing a difficulty

_____ when things are going well

_____ in church

_____ an ongoing conversation with God throughout the day

_____ when you are alone
_____ when you are with other Christians

3. When you pray, which are you more likely to do?

_____ pray a prayer from memory such as the Lord's Prayer

_____ read a prayer from a book of prayers

_____ read a psalm or hymn stanza as a prayer

_____ put your own thoughts in your own words

_____ write out your prayers or prayer topics in journal form

_____ a combination of

4. What, if anything, would you like to change about your prayer life?

5. Specifically, what will you need to do to bring about these changes?

To Do at Home

1. Establish a personal prayertime and prayer place.

2. Daily, pray with and for your children and for your family's specific needs.

3. Purchase and read a book of prayers for mothers.

4. Keep a prayer journal. Encourage your older

children to do the same. Simply record dates, prayer topics, and/or whole prayers. Reading them later is a powerful reminder of how God answers our prayers in His wise ways.

Closing Prayer

Allow one person or group to read the Leader sections. All others respond with the Response sections.

Leader: Lord, thank You for this chance to grow in my relationship with and understanding of You and Your Word.

Response: Help me to continue to grow. Keep me aware of Your presence and power in my life.

Leader: Thank You, Lord, for sending Jesus to be my Savior and for Your Spirit's pleadings and groanings on my behalf.

Response: Encourage me in my parenting and bring me to pray to You often for my children.

Leader: Thank You for being a Father who always has the time and patience to listen to every word I pray, and so we again join to pray!

All: Our Father in heaven, hallowed be Your name, Your kingdom come, Your will be done on earth as in heaven. Give us today our daily bread. Forgive us our sins as we forgive those who sin against us. Lead us not into temptation, but deliver us from evil. For the kingdom, the power, and the glory are Yours now and forever. Amen.

Leaders Notes

Session 1

A Mother Is a Daughter

▲ Focus

Welcome everyone. Give each participant a copy of the Study Guide. Encourage participants to write their names on the front covers. Ask that they take the booklets home between sessions and bring them back each time the group meets.

▲ Objectives

That by the power of the Holy Spirit working through God's Word the participants will

1. reflect upon the parenting they received as it influences their own parenting;

2. forgive their parents for whatever was not right, admirable, or excellent;

3. look to God the Father as the perfect parent who will forgive them and empower them to honor Him in their parenting.

▲ Opening Prayer

Ask participants to join you in praying the words of the prayer printed in the Study Guide.

▲ Focusing Our Attention

Read the italicized section aloud to the group to set the initial tone for the study. Then invite participants to introduce themselves to the others in the group, briefly sharing information about the mother or mother-figure in their lives. Next discuss the statement in item 2. Encourage participants to share how their perspective on parenting changed when they became parents.

▲ Focusing on the Issue

Ask a volunteer to read the narrative about Kathy and her mother aloud to the group. Continue with a whole-group discussion of the questions. Possible responses follow.

1. Kathy's life as a daughter seems to be very much interfering with her life as a mother. In a sense she is trying to be to her children the kind of mother she needs, rather than the kind of mother they need. While it is important for her to express her love for her children openly, it is equally important for her to discipline them. Her fear of not being loved is making it difficult for her to be the strong mother she needs to be.

2. Although Kathy cannot change her mother, she can change herself. Kathy can ask for the Holy Spirit's power to focus on the raising of her children rather than on the negativity and undoing of her own childhood. Participants may suggest that Kathy should express her love to her mother and disregard possible consequences.

3. If Kathy's mother suddenly and unexpectedly expressed her love for her, Kathy would likely become more confident; however, Kathy's mothering skills will not improve without some intentional effort or planned intervention.

▲ Focusing on God's Word

Divide participants into small groups to discuss the questions in this section. After allowing several minutes for discussion, reassemble everyone into a large group and briefly review each item.

1. God's love for those who are His supersedes even the powerful love of parents for their children. He places people in families so that they might love and care for one another as He loves and cares for us.

2. God the Father is like our earthly fathers and mothers in that He loves us, protects us, cares for and about us. He too gave us life. He is different from our earthly parents because He is perfect, He loves us with a perfect love, He always knows what is best for us, He is all powerful, He will never die, and He is always with us.

3. Earthly families can keep us from feeling lonely by sharing God's love with us, spending time with us, and helping us to face life's daily challenges.

4. As His Holy Spirit works in us through Word and Sacrament, God desires His children to grow in faith so that Christ will fill us with His love and make us Christlike in our attitudes and actions.

▲ Focusing on My Life

Invite a participant to read the thoughts on Christian motherhood aloud to the group. Then continue as a whole group discussing the items that follow.

1. Assure everyone of the forgiveness for parenting failures and all other sins earned by Jesus through His perfect life and substitutionary death for us. The penalty has been paid. We are now free to forgive ourselves for what we have done and others for the wrongs they have committed against us.

2. Encourage participants to complete this item independently and privately. Tell them that while they need not write anything down, identifying and naming specific things that trouble them and then forgiving in Jesus' name those who have wronged them can bring peace and healing. When everyone is ready, pray aloud the prayer included in the Student Guide.

3. Tell participants that now we are going to focus on the good aspects of the parenting they received as children. After once again allowing time for participants to complete this section individually, encourage them to share with the group one or more of the things they wrote. Mention that these are things for which we can thank God as we make a conscious attempt to carry them into our parenting.

4. Affirm participant responses.

5. Again encourage participants to share and affirm their responses.

▲ To Do at Home

Encourage participants to do one or more of these activities during the coming week.

▲ Closing Prayer

Conclude this section as suggested in the Study Guide. Note that each session concludes with the Lord's Prayer and that it has been printed out to avoid the embarrassment that may occur when different versions are known by different members. Point out the prayer is addressed to our Father. His fathering wisdom will both instruct and draw together the members of the group just as His perfect parenting will guide us throughout the course.

Session 2

A Mother Is a Mother

▲ Focus

Welcome everyone. Make sure each participant has a copy of the Study Guide. Encourage participants to write their names on the front covers. Ask that they take the booklets home between sessions and bring them back each time the group meets.

▲ Objectives

That by the power of the Holy Spirit working through God's Word the participants will
1. recognize the unique role God has designed for mothers within the structure of the family;
2. thank Jesus for the difference His forgiveness, guidance, and power bring to the lives of those desiring to honor Him in their parenting;
3. demonstrate a desire to love and care for their children as a grateful response to all God has done for them in Christ Jesus.

▲ Opening Prayer

Pray the prayer printed in the Study Guide or lead the group in an extemporaneous prayer.

▲ Focusing Our Attention

Use this activity to get the group off and running. Allow several minutes for them to share with a partner or in small groups about their childhood.

▲ Focusing on the Issue

Invite several volunteers to read the account of Rhonda, taking turns, paragraph by paragraph. Then ask participants to work in pairs or groups of three or four to respond to the questions. After several minutes, reassemble the large group and briefly review each question.

1. Answers may vary. Evidence of a good relationship may be found in Lindsay's willingness to tell her mother what is bothering her. Lindsay also seems pleased with many aspects of her mother's mothering. Rhonda obviously cares a great deal about Lindsay and her feelings or she would not make them such a priority.

2. A mother can be a lifelong friend; however, a mother must also be able to display authority and maturity. A mother's friendship for her child has a deeper dimension than the friendship enjoyed among peers.

3. Answers will vary. Perhaps Rhonda's relationship with Lindsay would benefit from formulating a mutually agreed upon plan for Rhonda's involvement with Lindsay's friends. Especially while in these often difficult and insecure early teen years, Lindsay needs the assurance that her mother's primary devotion is to her.

4. Encourage discussion by sharing one or more ways in which you would have finished these statements. Some of these responses may even be humorous in retrospect. Sharing and participation in this section must always be optional depending on the participant's comfort level.

5. Chances are, most of these idealistic vows have not been kept. Perhaps keeping some of them would not have been advisable since most were made without the benefit of maturity and wisdom.

6. a. This parent is giving the teen permission to ignore the law. By undermining another's authority, the parent is also undermining his or her own authority. These words may teach a child that obedience is optional and conditional rather than expected.

b. While undermining the teacher's authority, this parent is also giving the permission to fail. It would be wiser to offer to help the child.

c. The parent is giving the child permission to put God's natural laws aside. By refusing to take a hard line, this parent is condoning and perhaps even encouraging dangerous and immoral behavior.

d. This parent is demeaning the bus driver, an authority figure to the child, in the child's presence. Though most likely done thoughtlessly and in anger, this approach is destroying respect instead of teaching obedience.

Mention that just as those whose failings are evidenced in these quotes, all of us sometimes fail in our parenting.

Conclude this section emphasizing the all-encompassing forgiveness Jesus has earned for us through His life, death, and resurrection.

▲ Focusing on a Mother's Role

Begin this section by reading the beginning paragraph aloud to the group. Continue with a discussion of the numbered items as a whole group activity, inviting participants to share insights each item provides on the unique role of motherhood. Although answers may vary somewhat, they may resemble the following.

1a. As parents, mothers have the privilege of telling the Good News of Jesus and of living and witnessing their faith to the children God has given them. Although people cannot take anything with them when they leave this world, down through the centuries many godly children have followed their parents into heavenly glory because of the saving faith that was transmitted from generation to generation.

b. Just as Hannah prayed to God for her son Samuel, she dedicated him to the Lord. Similarly, by faith women of God pray for their children and instruct them in the truth so that by faith they, like Samuel, will give their whole lives over to the Lord.

c. This passage from Proverbs identifies a woman who fears the Lord as the most praiseworthy and noble of all women.

2a. This child's comments illustrate the time-honored understanding that a mother makes a house into a home, a group of people into a family. The presence of a loving mother makes the home a happy, secure place.

b. A Christian mother can play a most significant role in a child's spiritual nurture—perhaps greater than any other person in the life of a child.

c. Luther identifies motherhood as a highly honored role.

d. Through their words of praise, encouragement, and guidance, mothers can help open the doors of the future for their children as they excite their children with the possibilities God may have in store for them and pray that God will guide and direct them throughout their lives according to His will.

▲ To Do at Home

Encourage participants to do one or more of these activities during the week ahead.

▲ Closing Prayer

Encourage participants to join you in praying the closing prayer provided in the Study Guide.

Session 3

A Mother Is Forgiven and Forgiving

▲ Focus

Welcome everyone. Make sure each participant has a copy of the Study Guide. Encourage participants to write their names on the front covers. Ask that they take the booklets home between sessions and bring them back each time the group meets.

▲ Objectives

That by the power of the Holy Spirit working through God's Word the participants will

1. be reminded that God, through Christ's death and resurrection, forgave the sins of all mankind;

2. recognize opportunities to ask for and share God's forgiveness;

3. model Christ's forgiveness in their relationships with others.

▲ Opening Prayer

Invite participants to join you in praying the prayer printed in the Study Guide, or lead the group in an extemporaneous prayer thanking God for His goodness in Christ Jesus and asking the Holy Spirit's blessing upon your study of this lesson.

▲ Focusing Our Attention

Ask participants to do this activity, sharing with a partner or with three or four others in a small group.

▲ Focusing Our Sights

Invite a volunteer to read aloud the italicized true story that begins this section. Then continue with a discussion of the questions that follow. Allow participants to discuss the questions in small groups. Then reassemble the whole group and briefly review responses for each question.

1. Forgetting is a part of forgiving. When God forgives our sins, He no longer holds them against us in any way. Even if we remember someone's wrongdoing, our forgetting process can be helped by making it a family rule not to discuss past infractions.

2. Keeping track of a child's sins and continually reminding him or her of them may hamper the development of the child's self-esteem. This type of forgetting, however, does not preclude parents from remembering incidents from the past for the purpose of assisting and monitoring the growth and development of the child's character.

3. In Christ there is always forgiveness. True repentance, however, includes a desire to turn from sin. Nevertheless, no matter how many times a sin is committed, forgiveness is always freely available because of the death and resurrection of Jesus Christ.

▲ Focusing on the Issue

Invite one or more volunteers to read aloud the italicized account that begins this section. Continue discussing the questions in this section as a whole group.

1. The best way to teach a child to say "I'm sorry" is for the parent to model that behavior in his or her relationships.

2. This mother and son helped each other to feel forgiven by quietly nestling and hugging one another. Affirm additional suggestions for ways to help children feel forgiven.

▲ Focusing on God's Word

Invite participants to complete the discussion questions in this section in pairs or in small groups with three or four. After allowing time for them to work through all the items, reassemble everyone and briefly review their responses.

1. Jesus' forgiveness is immediate and unconditional. Forgiveness cannot be earned; Jesus earned it once and for all. Now it is a free gift we have the joy of sharing.

2. God desires the forgiveness Christ has earned for us to be the foundation for our relationship with Him as well as the focus for our relationships with others. Although the world often advises to repay evil for evil, God says, "Forgive, as, in Christ, you have been forgiven."

3. a. The forgiveness earned for us by Jesus empowers Christians to forgive others.

b. As the power of the Gospel takes root in each forgiven heart, individuals are moved by the Holy Spirit to forgive those who have offended them and more and more lives are touched with Christ's forgiveness and love.

▲ Focusing on My Life

Encourage participants to work through the items in this section independently. After approximately three to five minutes, invite general comments or reflections on the subjects of forgiveness and forgiving as they relate to parenting.

▲ To Do at Home

Encourage participants to do one or more of these activities during the week ahead.

69

▲ Closing Prayer

Conclude the session praying the responsive prayer printed in the Study Guide

Session 4

A Mother Is Loved and Loving

▲ Focus

Welcome everyone. Make sure each participant has a copy of the Study Guide. Encourage participants to write their names on the front covers. Ask that they take the booklets home between sessions and bring them back each time the group meets.

▲ Objectives

That by the power of the Holy Spirit working through God's Word the participants will

1. affirm that they are infinitely, intimately, and eternally loved by God;

2. recognize and desire to make use of opportunities to share God's love with their families;

3. ask for God's help in learning to practice consistent, unconditional love.

▲ Opening Prayer

Invite participants to join you in praying the prayer printed in the Study Guide or lead the group in an extemporaneous prayer, thanking God for His goodness in Christ Jesus and asking the Holy Spirit's blessing upon your study of this lesson.

▲ Focusing Our Attention

Invite participants to share with a partner or in small groups the evidence of their parents' love they remember most.

▲ Focusing on the Issue

Read the italicized portion of this section aloud to the group. Then continue with a discussion of the questions that follow.

1–2. Participants are likely to identify with Marilyn. Encourage them to share freely; however, don't force anyone to share.

▲ Focusing on God's Word

Invite volunteers to take turns reading the material in this section, paragraph by paragraph. Pause between paragraphs to add your insights or to explain or reinforce the information just read. Ask participants to work in pairs or in groups of three or four to complete the questions in this section. Then reassemble everyone for a brief review of responses for each item.

1. a. Just as God's love covers over our human flaws and failings, in Christ parents can ask for and receive forgiveness from their children. Children will feel safe, secure, and confident in spite of their parents' failings as long as they know they are loved by them.

b. God's love for us in Christ Jesus is the source of a Christian's love for all others—including the other members of their family. We love because He first loved us.

c. Because of Jesus we can confess our sins to one another as to God and find release in the forgiveness that is ours in Him.

d. Our God is a God of action. Working through the Gospel as we receive its power through Word and Sacrament, God's Spirit moves us to perform acts of love even when we don't feel like it. From these acts of love, the feeling of love will emerge later from within the giver as God's power takes hold.

2. Emphasize that the description of love found in 1 Corinthians 13 identifies the pure love of Christ for us—a

love that by His power also we have for others. Accept participant responses that resemble the following.

LOVE IS …	LOVE ISN'T …
patient	envious
kind	boastful
protective	proud
trusting	self-seeking
hopeful	concerned about keeping a
persevering	record of wrongs
sincere	delighted by evil
encouraging	
humble	
more interested in others than self	

3. God's Word suggests that we extend His love to others by sharing with those in need and by practicing hospitality.

▲ Love in Action

Read or invite a volunteer to read the material in this section aloud to the group. Ask participants to work with partners or with two or three others in small groups to discuss questions 1–3. Then reassemble everyone for a brief review of the small group discussions. Allow time for participants to respond to items 4 and 5 privately.

1. Many families have some unique ways to say "I love you." It may be holding hands while praying and giving a squeeze at the conclusion of the prayer. It may involve the use of special nicknames. Encourage participants to share their traditions and suggestions.

2. Encourage participants to respond to these words and to share what they have added.

3. Sometimes love demonstrates itself in actions that appear authoritarian or restrictive but are motivated out of love and concern for the recipient.

4–5. Introduce items 4 and 5 by saying that sometimes each of us feels unloved and unappreciated by those we care about most. Assure participants that it is not unusual for a mother to feel unloved. Often a mother is so intent on helping family members to feel loved and accepted that her own feelings are subdued and bypassed. Encourage participant sharing of ways mothers can communicate their desire and need for a more open display of affection from their families.

Parents sometimes hear "You don't love me!" statements. Invite suggestions as to how these statements might best be handled. Suggest that if a parent responds with a defensive, "What do you mean I don't love you? After all the things I do for you ...," communication may only break down further. Simply saying, "I do love you and I always will" or calmly asking, "Why do you feel I don't love you?" can lead to improved communication. Invite comments or insights generated from items 4 and 5, but don't force anyone to share.

▲ To Do at Home

Encourage participants to do one or more of these activities during the week ahead.

▲ Closing Prayer

Conclude the session by praying the responsive prayer provided in the Study Guide.

Session 5

A Mother Teaches and Is Taught

▲ Focus

Welcome everyone. Make sure each participant has a copy of the Study Guide. Encourage participants to write their names on the front covers. Ask that they take the booklets home after this session and bring them back for the final session.

▲ Objectives

That by the power of the Holy Spirit working through God's Word the participants will

1. identify Jesus Christ as their lifelong Teacher;

2. recognize and make the most of opportunities to teach His Word to their children;

3. identify lessons God has taught them through the children He has given them.

▲ Opening Prayer

Ask participants to join you in praying the words of the prayer printed in the Study Guide.

▲ Focusing Our Attention

Read or invite a volunteer to read the italicized account aloud to the class. Ask participants to work with a partner or in small groups of three or four to share lessons they have learned from the children in their lives.

▲ Focusing on the Issue

Have participants remain with their partners or in small groups to work through this section. Ask each group to appoint someone to read the introductory material aloud to the group. Then have them continue with a discussion of the questions. After allowing ample time for discussion, reassemble everyone for a brief, item by item review. Answers may vary.

1. By Maggie's actions her children may learn to become insecure, developing an unhealthy fear of the world as frightening place in which to live.

2. As the children of Betty and Mike are continually exposed to the means of grace, God's Spirit remains at work in their lives, strengthening them in the saving faith.

3. Protecting children from the negative aspects of life deprives them of the opportunity to learn how to meet and cope with difficulties. Wilma's approach may cause her children to either have unrealistic expectations about life or to be inadequately prepared to deal with life's problems.

4. When we join children in learning to know and apply God's loving will and His ways, we give our loving God the place He desires to occupy in the life of the family.

5. Keeping the lines of communication open is vital to the growth of healthy family relationships.

▲ The Most Important Thing to Learn

Continue with the section, using the same approach as in the previous section.

1. Those who trust in Jesus have forgiveness of sins plus a new and eternal life that begins at the time an individual comes to faith. With the apostle Paul, believers can rejoice that our citizenship is in heaven (Philippians 3:20).

2. a. Christian parents of today "tie ... symbols on [our] hands and bind them on [our] foreheads" by wearing Christian symbols fashioned into jewelry or as emblems on clothing such as T-shirts, sweatshirts, and caps. We "write them on the doorframes of [our] houses and on [our] gates" by placing Christian literature, music, plaques, and pictures in our homes. In addition to reading and discussing God's Word and worshiping and praying together, these actions help to reinforce the important place Christ occupies in the home.

b. Making the things of God a top priority in the Christian home will provide opportunity for the entire family to derive strength and joy from God through His Word.

c. The Christian home can help root children in the Word of God through which God guides, empowers, and encourages those who belong to Him.

d. Through His Word, God equips His children for lives of service to Him, showing us the most healthy and successful way in which to live.

e. God's grace as it is at work in the Christian home builds the discernment and self-control so necessary among the people of God as they function and share the Good News in our sinful world.

3. a. This situation provides an excellent opportunity for the parent to share his or her own faith in Jesus, to pray with Jim for the family of his friend, and to discuss the importance of trusting in God when facing the hurts, tragedies, and unanswerable questions of life.

b. A parent might use this opportunity to talk about God as the maker, preserver, and ruler of the entire universe and everything in it. The parent might point out that the theory of evolution directs the attention away from God the creator to center it upon man as the highest entity on the evolutionary ladder. He or she might help the daughter to recognize that those who see themselves as mere products of a random occurrence disregard what God's Word teaches about people as specially chosen, created, and redeemed by Christ crucified.

c. This conversation provides an opportunity to talk openly about God and all He has done for us and the value of joining together with others to worship and learn more about Him. A wise parent will also investigate to learn the specific reasons for the boy's complaints and see what can be done to help him appreciate and look forward to Sunday school.

d. Answering this question gives parents the opportunity to explain what God says in His Word on this issue and to affirm His love and forgiveness for those who repent of their disobedience.

e. Parents will need to deal with the matter of deliberate disobedience of the rule. Children benefit from learning that breaking rules results in negative consequences. Repentance of the wrong provides parents with the opportunity to share with their children the Good News of the forgiveness available freely to all through Christ Jesus.

▲ Focusing on My Life

Ask participants to complete this section independently. After allowing ample time for them to think through and respond to these items, invite comments or insights from the group.

▲ To Do at Home

Encourage participants to do one or more of these activities during the coming week.

▲ Closing Prayer

Conclude the session with the closing prayer provided in the Study Guide.

Session 6

A Mother Prays and Is Prayed For

▲ Focus

Welcome everyone to the final session of this course. Make sure each participant has a copy of the Study Guide. Briefly review the topics covered in the preceding five sessions.

▲ Objectives

That by the power of the Holy Spirit working through God's Word the participants will

1. acknowledge that God's Spirit is always interceding for them;

2. explore the role of prayer in the life of a Christian parent;

3. establish opportunities to pray with and for the members of their family.

▲ Opening Prayer

Invite participants to join you in praying the prayer printed in the Study Guide, or lead the group in an extemporaneous prayer thanking God for His goodness in Christ Jesus and asking the Holy Spirit's blessing upon the final session of this study.

▲ Focusing Our Attention

Invite participants to share with partners or in small groups about the means of communication from which they have received the most valuable information during the past 24 hours.

▼

▲ Focusing on the Issue

Read or ask a volunteer to read the introductory material in this section aloud to the group. Invite participants to respond to items 1 and 2 individually. Then have participants work in pairs or in groups of three or four to discuss items 3–5. After allowing time for discussion, reassemble everyone for a brief review of each item.

3. a. David calls on God because He knows God will always answer him. David asks God for protection from his enemies. Today, we continue to ask God's protection from our enemies, including the devil, the world, and our own sinful flesh.

b. These words, rewritten from a mother's perspective might be: "Lord, keep my child as the apple of Your eye. Protect him/her and guide him/her so the evils and enemies in our world can't hurt him/her."

4. None of our children really belong to us. They are all God's children, on loan to us to love, nurture, and raise in the knowledge of the Lord.

5. a. God promises to hear and answer those prayers offered in the name of Jesus.

b. God promises to answer our prayers according to our ultimate best interest when we pray according to His will.

c. God provides peace to those who approach life's difficulties and problems, committing them to God in prayer and offering them with thankfulness for God's many blessings to us.

d. A Christian family is one of those groups of two or three (or more) gathered together in the name of Christ. He promises to remain among them.

▲ Focusing on My Life

Read or paraphrase the introductory paragraph to the group. Then ask participants to discuss the items in this section in pairs or in groups of three or four. Reassemble everyone for a brief review of each item.

1. As God's Spirit works in Christian families through the Word, parents and children live out various responses to the Gospel in areas including stewardship, evangelism, service, fellowship, and worship.

2. From parents children learn to show love and concern for others as it has been shown to them.

▼

3. Stages of parenting differ according to the age of the children. Parents of any age can bring their petitions and prayers of thanksgiving on behalf of their children before their Father in heaven.

4. As with many aspects of nurture, children learn about spiritual things from what they see their parents doing as well as from what their parents say to them.

5. God strengthens the bond of family members as a side benefit of coming together to read and meditate upon God's Word and to offer prayers and praise to God.

▲ The Importance of Communication

Read or paraphrase the opening paragraph to the group. Then invite participants to respond individually to the items in this section. After several minutes, invite participants to share any thoughts or insights they may have after responding to these items.

▲ To Do at Home

Encourage participants to do one for more of these activities in the immediate future.

▲ Closing Prayer

Thank participants for joining you for this study. Conclude with the responsive prayer included in the Study Guide.